9

MORE

TO

REMEMBER

BOOKS BY DUDLEY RANDALL

POEM COUNTERPOEM
(with Margaret Danner)

FOR MALCOLM
Poems on the Life and the Death of Malcolm X
(edited with Margaret G. Burroughs)

CITIES BURNING

BLACK POETRY
A Supplement to Anthologies Which Exclude Black Poets (editor)

LOVE YOU

MORE TO REMEMBER
Poems of Four Decades

MORE
TO
REMEMBER

POEMS OF FOUR DECADES

by

Dudley Randall

wTp

THIRD WORLD PRESS

Chicago   Illinois

ACKNOWLEDGEMENTS

Some of these poems have previously appeared in *Beloit Poetry Journal, Black Arts Anthology, Black Expression, Broadside Posters, The Chicago Tribune, The Detroit News, Essence, Fisk Herald, Free Lance, Journal of Black Poetry, Negro Digest, Negro History Bulletin, Peninsula Poets, Tan,* and *Ten: A Detroit Anthology.*

Cover by Shirley Woodson

LCN: 75-141237
ISBN: Paper O-910296-58-8 $1.95
ISBN: Cloth O-910296-58-8 $5.00

Manufactured in the United States of America

TO DON L. LEE

A STRONG NEW VOICE POINTING THE WAY

Contents

1

THE KINDNESS AND THE CRUELTY

For Pharish Pinckney,
   Bindle-Stiff During the Depression   15

Vacant Lot   16

Ghetto Girls   17

Laughter in the Slums   18

Winter Campus: Ann Arbor   19

Shape of the Invisible   20

Nocturne   21

2

INCREDIBLE HARVESTS

Our Name for You   25

Separation   26

Rx   27

The Line-Up   28

Jailhouse Blues   29

The Apparition   30

Perspectives   31

Spring before a War   32

Helmeted Boy   33

Football Season   34

Lost in the Mails   35

Pacific Epitaphs   36

   Rabaul   36

   New Georgia   36

   Treasury Islands   36

   Palawan   36

   Espiritu Santu   37

   Iwo Jima   37

   Bismarck Sea   37

   Tarawa   37

   Halmaherra   37

   New Guinea   38

   Luzon   38

   Coral Sea   38

   Bougainville   38

   Vella Vella   39

   Leyte   39

   Guadalcanal   39

   Borneo   39

The Ascent   40

Coral Atoll   41

The Leaders   42

3

IF NOT ATTIC, ALEXANDRIAN

Interview   45

The Dilemma   48

Aim   49

Love Song   50

April Mood   51

Anniversary Words   52

4

AND HER SKIN DEEP VELVET NIGHT

Poet   55

Aphorisms   56

Hymn   57

The Trouble with Intellectuals   58

The Intellectuals   59

Poem, on a Nude, from the Ballet, to Debussy's
   Prelude *L'Après-Midi D'un Faune,* after
   Mallarmé's *L'Après-Midi D'un Faune*   60

Justice   61

Mainly by the Music   62

Langston Blues   63

Straight Talk from a Patriot   64

Daily News Report   65

Seeds of Revolution   66

An Answer to Lerone Bennett's Questionnaire
 On A Name for Black Americans   67

Nationalist   69

Put Your Muzzle Where Your Mouth Is   70

Informer   71

F.B.I. Memo   72

Abu   73

The Militant Black Poet   74

Sniper   75

Ancestors   76

On Getting a Natural   77

PREFACE

Because of the nature of my two previous books, many poems had to be omitted. *Poem Counterpoem* included only poems which could be paired with Margaret Danner's. *Cities Burning* was limited to poems about this disintegrating era. This book is inclusive, containing poems selected from those written from the 1930's through the 1960's.

Here are the ways I was. Warts and all.

Now I feel free to strike off in other directions.

—Dudley Randall
Chicago, 1970

1
The
Kindness
and
the Cruelty

For Pharish Pinckney,
Bindle-Stiff During the Depression

You'd wake at morning, stiff from the hard floor
of rattling box car in a swaying train,
and wave at girls you'd never seen before
in little towns you'd never see again.

You felt the joy of roaming far and free,
and in the jungle shared the hobo's stew,
and learned the kindness and the cruelty
of the land that mothered and rejected you.

Vacant Lot

Crouched in its giant green the Indian hid
And on the trapper sprang the ambuscade.
It was the wilderness to city kid,
And paradise to each pariah weed.

We'd give the slip to megaphone-voiced wardens
For atavistic field where memories blur,
As asters make their getaway from gardens
And scrape acquaintance with the uncultured burr.

There, among sunflowers, goldenrod and thistle,
We'd act the old drama of boys' strength,
Bloody each other's noses, blacken eyes, and wrestle
Till hustled home to bed by moon at length.

While April set us sprinting round the bases,
October chasing the eccentric ball,
December sculpturing farcial forms and faces,
It was chameleon stage containing all.

Ghetto Girls

With ivory, saffron, cinnamon, chocolate faces,
Glowing with all the hues of all the races;
Lips laughing, generous-curved, vermilion-tinted,
Lips of a child, but, like a woman's, painted;
Eyes where the morning stars yet glimmer on;
Feet swift to dance through juke-box nights till dawn:

> *Little girls, young, and foolish-wise,*
> *Flaunting knowledge in your ignorant eyes,*
> *You are like flowers that bud, then droop away,*
> *Or like the bright, quick-darkened tropic day.*
> *Lovers and kisses, cruel, careless, light,*
> *Will you remember down the long, deep night?*

Laughter in the Slums

In crippled streets where happiness seems buried
under the sooty snow of northern winter,
sudden as bells at twilight,
bright as the moon, full as the sun, there blossoms
in southern throats rich flower of flush fields
hot with the furnace sun of Georgia Junes,
laughter that cold and blizzards cannot kill.

Winter Campus: Ann Arbor

April took flesh in clear September air
when one girl paused upon the colonnade,
turned, and for a heartbeat hovered there
while yellow elm leaves drifted past her hair.

Here, now, the same soft youngness is conveyed
as these bareheaded throngs stream to and fro
with footfalls noiseless in the sudden snow,
a hum like bees pulsating on and on
while treble voices tremble in the air
and rime with chiming of the carillon.

Shape of the Invisible

At dawn
Upon the snow
The delicate imprint
Left by the sleeping body of
The wind.

Nocturne

Light has laid down its chisel.
Only a staring, mutilated moon
crawls over the dim meadows of the mind
where my love lies irrevocably lost,
beyond the clasp of pity or desire.

In recollection's mists her face is blurred,
and she has left no spoor
except, perhaps, in caverns of a dream,
or in the insinuations of a willow.

2

Incredible Harvests

Our Name for You
(For my daughter)

Baby, born only yesterday —
    Name yet to choose,
We wish your tiny lips could say
    What name to use.

Shall we name you after a flower, sweet girl, —
    Violet or *Rose*?
Or after a jewel — *Ruby, Pearl,*
    For your skin that glows?

Shall we call you *Constance, Prudence, Faith?*
    From the storied dead
Select a name like a laurel wreath
    For your little head?

Barbara, Ardis, Ruth, Germaine
    Are a singing few.
In years to come may you not complain
    Of our name for you.

Separation

She's going away
Without telling where.
She refuses to stay,
She's going away
Though so many pray
And so many care.
She's going away,
Without telling where.

$$R_X$$

Love's a disease that's difficult to cure;
but purgatives of tears may have some power,
with regimen of loneliness, denial,
deceitfulness and falsehood and betrayal.
Injections of contempt may hasten health,
or daily immersions in a bath of filth.

And yet this maddening malady may linger
in spite of being cauterized with anger.
Even disillusion's sulfanilamide
against this sickness may give little aid.
So the remedy that proves the surest at last
is mould in the mouth and worms within the breast.

The Line-Up

Elegantly we sit for portrait,
Are measured for our height and weight,
and scrutinized for any more trait
that marks us off from those who're straight.

This fellow has committed murder,
and he's regarded with respect,
this pimply youngster is a burglar,
and this old man shows girls his sex.

No one has taken (how we're flattered)
such interest in us before.
It almost seems as if we mattered,
although it's something of a bore

to take the stage pursued with laughter
and questions on the fact, cause, time,
and leave, for generations after,
fingerprints in files of crime.

Jailhouse Blues

I wish I was lyin
wrapped in my woman's arms.
O I wish I was lyin
safe in my woman's arms.
Then I wouldn't study to
do no one no harm.

I can get all the whisky
and gin that I can drink,
best Canadian whisky
and gin that I can drink.
I pour it down faster
than water runs down the sink.

I got a big radio
that plays ten records straight,
a fine big radio
plays ten records straight,
and a wide soft bed for
me and my lovin mate.

I got three women
to love me day and night,
black, brown and yellow
to love me day and night.
When I leave this jailhouse,
I'm sure gonna treat 'em right.

The Apparition

To my sleep at night there comes a constant guest.
His eyes, deeper than any woman's eyes
that ever burned in mine, destroy my rest.
His voice, knifing and vibrant as the cries
of lovers at the summit of delight,
calls out my name with more than lovers' passion,
while his pale hands, that drip blood in the night,
reach to embrace me in forgiving fashion.

Perspectives

Futile to chide the stinging shower
or prosecute the thorn
or set a curse upon the hour
in which my love was born.

All's done, all's vanished, like a sail
that's dwindled down the bay.
Even the mountains vast and tall
the sea dissolves away.

Spring before a War

Spring came early that year.
Early the snow melted and crocuses took over
And in dooryard gardens blossomed the flower of the
    slain Greek boy.
Before the spring retired came roses
And orange lilies and great blanched spheres of peonies.
Days were warm and bright and fields promised incredible
    harvests,
And in meadows fresh and unscarred
With waists encircled and flanks touching
Strolled the dead boys
And the widowed girls.

Helmeted Boy

Your forehead capped with steel
Is smoother than a coin
With profile of a boy who fell
At Marathon.

Football Season

Now in the evenings rose and cool,
Tall above shadowed emerald grass,
With passion never given to school
Boys linger late to kick and pass.

Beneath their feet the green blades yield,
And seem, by some grave twilight change,
Familiar gridiron, lot, or field,
   And not the rifle range.

Lost in the Mails

Dear Sun

I Will anser your letter was glad to here from you
Mom didden wont you to go off Sun i got your Birth
Stefike back from coat House honey you rite me often
for i Sure worrie over you going off from home. Sis
& Baby is O K. tell Murray to rite to i close anser Soon

Love mother

Pacific Epitaphs

Rabaul

In far-off Rabaul
I died for democracy.
Better I fell
In Mississippi.

New Georgia

I loved to talk of home.
Now I lie silent here.

Treasury Islands

I mastered the cards,
The dice obeyed me.
But I could not palm
The number on the bullet.

Palawan

Always the peacemaker,
I stepped between
One buddy armed with an automatic
And another with a submachine gun.

Espiritu Santu

I hated guns,
Was a poor marksman,
But struck one target.

Iwo Jima

Like oil of Texas
My blood gushed here.

Bismarck Sea

Under the tossing foam
This boy who loved to roam
Makes his eternal home.

Tarawa

Tell them this beach
Holds part of Brooklyn.

Halmaherra

Laughing I left the earth.
Flaming returned.

New Guinea

A mosquito's tiny tongue
Told me a bedtime story.

Luzon

Splendid against the night
The searchlights, the tracers' arcs,
And the red flare of bombs
Filling the eye,
And the brain.

Coral Sea

In fluid element
The airman lies.

Bougainville

A spent bullet
Entered the abdominal cavity
At an angle of thirty-five degrees,
Penetrated the *pars pylorica,*
Was deflected by the *sternum,*
Pierced the *auricula dextra,*
And severed my medical career.

Vella Vella

The rope hugged tighter
Than the girl I raped.

Leyte

By twenty bolos hacked and beat,
He was a tender cut of meat.

Guadalcanal

Your letter.
These medals.
This grave.

Borneo

Kilroy
Is
Here.

The Ascent

Into the air like dandelion seed
Or like the spiral of lark into the light
Or fountain into sun. All former sight
From hill or mountain was a mere hint of this.
We gain a new dimension. What had been
Our prison, where we crawled and clung like ants,
We spurn, and vision lying far beneath us.

O naked shape of earth! What green mammelles,
Arteries of gold and silver, turquoise flanks,
Plush jungles now are patterned! As we bank,
The earth tilts; we are level and aloof,
And it spins on and on among the stars.
We poise in air, hang motionless, and see
The planet turn with slow grace of a dancer.

Coral Atoll

No wedding ring of doges, this white cirque that lies
dazzling, immaculate, upon the blue
of deep Pacific. High the airman sees
small ships crawl past it, and the surf exclaim
upon that O in foam less shining white.

No spiny island hurled out of the deep
by birthpangs of an earthquake is this round,
or green plateau that's sentient with warm life.
Things without thought, vision or dream,
through mute numb years under the swaying tides
have died into a perfect form that sings.

The Leaders

They are the shy, the gauche, the clumsy, the unfitted,
The solitary, withdrawn apart, the dissatisfied,
Inspiring the smile, the lifted eyebrow, indifference,
Or maligned in anger, stoned and driven out from the people.

Uncensored dreamers, thinkers of forbidden thoughts,
Saboteurs of temples, seekers after undiscovered territories,
They are our enemies, hostile to our traditions,
Diverting the ancient channels of our blood.

But in the day of terror and confusion
When we know not which way to turn
And the straight paths crook, and the monuments
Crumple,
We seek them in exile, we turn to them
As the source of our strength, as fathers
Who point out the way, and comfort
Those in distress, as brothers
Sharing our burden, and as seers
Conceiving all our beauty.

Then in the day when peace blooms over the earth
And all men are gods and makers,
Honor them, seed of this flower, sires of this birth.

3

If
Not Attic,
Alexandrian

Interview

What's going on there? Why the wrestling match?
Let go that fellow. Bring him here to me.

You're rather rumpled from this roughing up,
But otherwise in right good shape. And so
You crossed the moat and climbed the barbed-wire fence,
Escaped the dogs and dodged the guards' revolvers
And got this close to me with just a necktie
Twisted out of place, a swollen lip,
And rumpled coat that even now you're brushing
Back into shape. And how? Who did you bribe,
Flatter, browbeat or blackmail to crash in?
But never mind. I'll find that out. And someone
Will smart for that. But what are you doing here?
Are you another crackpot come to shoot me
Or pester me with plans to save the world?
You're a reporter, want an interview?

Isn't your editor satisfied with the statements
My staff mailed out about the new Foundation?
All of the facts were there: the greatest sum
Ever devoted to philanthropy

Donated for research in education,
Science and medicine to make life better.
My brightest boys devised that press release,
Full of the hokum that pleases the public best.
But you want more? My own ideas and views?

Well, I'm an old man, and a sick one too,
Or so these pill-men say, and seldom talk
For public hearing. (My advisers tell me
My tongue's too sharp.) But since you've been
    rough-handled
And seem a bold-faced youngster much like me
When I was your age, I'll talk frankly to you,
And what you think the public can digest
You're free to write. The rest, use for yourself.

Some say the Fund's to cheat the state of taxes.
Others, more kind, insist it's just a way
To pay back mankind what I've robbed them of.
They're all mistaken. What I want, I take.
And what I take, I keep. Why give it back?
I never thought the world was made for me.

It has its own laws, rolls along as merry
As if I were not here, nor ever had been.
So why should I complain if my toe's crushed?

What I have done is to observe its ways,
And having learned them, use them to advantage.
Are men dishonest, petty, greedy, vain?
Why should I pule and murmur if they are?
I'll use their greed and vanity to my ends,
Not snivel, try to reform the world, and fail.
I've used the world for what it is, and gained
A many million. Now it is my whim
To try to change the world, and prove to those
Who could not take the world just as they found it
And therefore lack the power to change it at all
That one old, greedy, and predacious villain
Can do more good in the world than all of them
In all their years of whining and complaining.
And, what is more, they'll be my instruments.

So here's my story. Use it as you want to.
You needn't send a galley. I'll get your name
From the signed article. And remember it.

The Dilemma
(My poems are not sufficiently obscure
To please the critics.

— Ray Durem)

I'd like to sing (but singing is naive)
To express emotion freely and unveiled,
(But should I wear my heart upon my sleeve,
And as a lush Romantic be assailed?)
And sometimes I would like to make a plain
Unvarnished statement bare of metaphor,
(But to speak simply is to be inane;
A man of the world should never be a bore.)

And so I cultivate my irony,
And search strange books for the recondite allusion.
The time's confused, so I must also be,
And in the reader likewise plant confusion.
So, though no Shelley, I'm a gentleman,
And, if not Attic, Alexandrian.

Aim

A rhythm that's as natural as the beat
which heart and pulse unconsciously repeat,

a melody that modulates the notes
emotion vibrates in a billion throats,

bodied in words transparent as the air,
which hint the whole by showing the part clear.

Love Song

Until the shadows go,
And morning gilds the copse,
Beloved, be like a doe
Upon the mountain tops.

As softly as the snow
Upon the mountain drops,
Your love on me bestow
Until the shadows go
And morning gilds the copse.

Beloved, be like a doe,
Upon the mountain tops.

April Mood

This is the season when, in days of old,
Young knights would don again their dinted arms,
And, as in tales at great length we are told,
Would venture forth through forests fields and farms
To rescue damsels from magicians' charms
And saucy worms exhaling sultry flame,
And out of hard encounters, fierce alarms
Would win eternal glory and a dame.
So, though I am not quite on fire for fame,
And though few ogres live upon my street,
Beloved, can you hold me much to blame
If in this month so stirring and so sweet
    Something extraordinary I wish to do
    To prove my valor, and my love for you?

Anniversary Words

You who have shared my scanty bread with me
and borne my carelessness and forgetfulness
with only occasional lack of tenderness,
who have long patiently endured my faculty
for genial neglect of practicality,
for forgetting the morning and the parting caress
and for leaving rooms in a great disorderliness
which when I entered were as neat as they could be,

despite the absent-mindedness of my ways
and the not seldom acerbity of your tone,
I sometimes catch a softness in your gaze
which tells me after all I am your own
and that you love me in no little way.
But I know it best by the things you never say.

4

And Her Skin Deep Velvet Night

Poet

Patron of pawn shops,
Sloppily dressed,
Bearded, hatless and graceless,
Reading when you should be working,
Fingering a poem in your mind
When you should be figuring a profit,
Convert to outlandish religions,
Zen, Ba'hai and Atheism,
Consorter with Negroes and Jews
And other troublesome elements
Who are always disturbing the peace
About something or other,
Friend of revolutionaries
And foe of the established order,
When will you slough off
This preposterous posture
And behave like a normal
Solid responsible
White Anglo Saxon Protestant?

Aphorisms

He who vilifies the Jew
next day will slander you.

He who calls his neighbor "nigger"
upon your turning back will snigger.

He who vaunts a Master Race
brings upon his line disgrace.

While he who calls a faith absurd
thrusts the spear into his Lord.

Hymn

Squat and ugly in your form,
but fierce as Moloch in your power,
accept our worship and our warm
dependence in this demon hour.

While problems of the world and state
knot up our minds with anguished choice,
yours is the power to extirpate
all cavil with volcanic voice.

And then no more of wrong or right,
or whose shrewd counsels we should keep.
One flash of sun-outshouting light,
and then the dark, forgetful sleep.

The Trouble with Intellectuals

The trouble with intellectuals
Is that they talk
T o o
M u c h.

Put an intellectual in bed with a woman
And instead of making love
He t a l k s
About love.
Put one in a living room and he wonders
Whether he's human
And whether he's alive,
Whereas the rest of us
Take for granted that we're human
And alive
And while the intellectual
T a l k s
We
L i v e.

The Intellectuals

The intellectuals talked.

They had to decide on principles.
Nothing should be done, nothing legislated
Till a rationale had been established.

The intellectuals talked.

Meanwhile the others,
Who believed in action,
And that they should be up and all the rest down,
Stormed the hall, shot the leaders and arrested the remainder,
Whom they later hanged.

Poem, on a Nude, from the Ballet, to Debussy's Prelude <u>L'Après-Midi D'un Faune</u>, after Mallarmé's <u>L'Apres-Midi D'un Faune</u>

—Dudley Randall
7 October 1967

Justice
(A Fable)

He fined the Wolf eleven cents
and gave the Lamb ten years in jail.

Mainly by the Music

Prisoned in cells of living,
We reach for sympathy
With words too gross and single
For full empathy,

And mainly by the music
That feelings subtly play
Upon these instruments of air
Does meaning find its way.

Langston Blues

Your lips were so laughing
Langston man
Your lips were so singing
Minstrel man
How death could touch them
Hard to understand

Your lips that laughed
And sang so well
Your lips that brought
Laughter from hell
Are silent now
No more to tell

So let us sing
A Langston blues
Sing a lost
Langston blues
Long-gone song
For Langston Hughes

Straight Talk from a Patriot

If the gooks in Viet Nam refuse to see
The virtue of our great democracy,
We'll make them see it — if we have to bomb
Or burn the whole damn country with napalm.

Daily News Report

We killed 250 men today.

We
   we *killed*
      we killed *two*
         we killed two *hundred*
            we killed two hundred *fifty*
               we killed two hundred fifty *men*
today

Today
   were living
      two
         two *hundred*
            two hundred *fifty*
               two hundred fifty *men*
were living
   today

Now they are dead
   We killed them
      We *killed*
         KILLED
            KILLED
them
   today

Seeds of Revolution

The Revolution
did not begin in 1966
when Stokely raised his fist
and shouted, Black Power.

Nor did it begin last year
when you read Fanon
and discovered you were black.

The Revolution was going on
when the first black
leaped overboard
to the sharks;

When blacks malingered,
or sabotaged the plantation,
or Tommed to outwit Ole Massa;

When your father (whom you deplore)
pushed a broom
and your mother (whom you despise)
scrubbed kitchens
so you could go to school
and read Fanon.

The Revolution
did not begin in 1966
when Stokely raised his fist
and shouted, Black Power.

Nor last year
when you read Fanon
and discovered you were black.

An Answer to
Lerone Bennett's Questionnaire
On A Name for Black Americans

Discarding the Spanish word for black
and taking the Anglo-Saxon word for Negro,
discarding the names of English slavemasters
and taking the names of Arabian slave-traders
won't put a single
bean in your belly
or an inch of steel
in your spine.

Call a skunk a rose,
and he'll still stink,
and make the name stink too.

Call a rose a skunk,
and it'll still smell sweet,
and even sweeten the name.

The spirit informs the name,
not the name the spirit.

If the white man took the name Negro,
and you took the name Caucasian,
he'd still kick your ass,
as long as you let him.

If you're so insecure
that a word makes you quake,
another word
won't cure you.

Change your mind,
not your name.

Change your life,
not your clothes.

Nationalist

"Black
is beautiful,"
he said,
as he stroked
her white
breasts.

Put Your Muzzle
Where Your Mouth Is
(or shut up)

KILL, KILL, KILL, he screamed.
But when I asked him
(naively, I suppose)
how many
he
had killed,
he said,
Not
1.

Informer

He shouted
"Black Power!"
so loudly
we never heard
his whispers
to the F.
B.
I.

F. B. I. Memo

The perfect spy
for the F. B. I.
must have:
beard
Afro
tiki
dashiki
Swahili
and cry
"Kill the honkies!"

Abu

Abu
's a stone black revolutionary.
Decided to blow up City Hall.
Put full-page ad
in *New York Times*
announcing his inten/
                    shun.
Says rightinfrontof
F.B.I. in fil/
              trators
he gon sassinate
rich white liberal
gave only *half*
a million
to N.A.A.C.P.
Says nothing 'bout that Southern sheriff
killed three black prisoners
'cept, he admire him
for his sin/
            cerity.

The Militant Black Poet

A militant black poet
read his scariest poems
to a literary club
of suburban white women.

After the reading
a white-haired lady commented
what a nice man he was,
and that in his place
she'd be much more bitter.

The militant black poet
went home
and *hanged* himself.

Sniper

Somewhere
On a rooftop
You fight for me.

Ancestors

Why are our ancestors
always kings or princes
and never the common people?

Was the Old Country a democracy
where every man was a king?
Or did the slavecatchers
steal only the aristocrats
and leave the fieldhands
laborers
streetcleaners
garbage collectors
dishwashers
cooks
and maids
behind?

My own ancestor
(research reveals)
was a swineherd,
who tended the pigs
in the Royal Pigstye
and slept in the mud
among the hogs.

Yet I'm as proud of him
as of any king or prince
dreamed up in fantasies
of bygone glory.

On Getting a Natural
(For Gwendolyn Brooks)

She didn't know she was beautiful,
though her smiles were dawn,
her voice was bells,
and her skin deep velvet Night.

She didn't know she was beautiful,
although her deeds,
kind, generous, unobtrusive,
gave hope to some,
and help to others,
and inspiration to us all. And
beauty is as beauty does,
they say.

Then one day there blossomed
a crown upon her head,
bushy, bouffant, real Afro-down,
Queen Nefertiti again.
And now her regal wooly crown
declares
I know
I'm black
AND
beautiful.

December 1969